DK Watch me grow

Rabbit

Contents

LONDON, NEW YORK, MUNICH,
MELBOURNE, and DELHI

Written and edited by Lisa Magloff
Designed by Sonia Whillock,
Mary Sandberg, and Pilar Morales

Publishing Manager Sue Leonard
Managing Art Editor Clare Shedden
Jacket Design Simon Oon
Picture Researcher Sarah Stewart-Richardson
Production Shivani Pandey
DTP Designer Almudena Díaz

First American Edition, 2004

Published in the United States by
DK Publishing, Inc.
375 Hudson Street
New York, New York 10014

04 05 06 07 08 10 9 8 7 6 5 4 3 2 1

ISBN 0-7566-0262-9

A Cataloging-in-Publication record for this book
is available from the Library of Congress.

Colour reproduction by Media, Development and Printing, Ltd.
Printed and bound in China by South China Printing Co. Ltd.

Discover more at

www.dk.com

4-5
I'm a rabbit

6-7
My mom and dad

8-9
Here is my home

10-11
Inside my family's nest

12-13
I'm getting curious

14-15
I'm four weeks old

16–17
I can find my own dinner

18–19
Now I'm grown up

20–21
The circle of life

22–23
My friends from
around the world

24
Glossary

I'm a rabbit

I have two large ears and a fluffy tail. My strong back legs help me to leap and run, and I am covered in soft fur to keep me warm.

A great sense of smell helps rabbits to sniff out danger.

Strong claws are good for digging.

This is my family.

Rabbits have many layers of thick fur.

Running away

Rabbits can run about as fast as you can ride your bicycle. This helps them outrun their enemies.

Wake up, everyone, it's time to get hopping.

My mom and dad

My mom and dad made their home under a large tree. They live with other rabbit families in a series of underground tunnels called a warren.

This is Dad.

This is Mom.

Saying hello
When rabbits meet, they say hello to each other by sniffing and touching noses.

This hole is an entrance tunnel.

Family facts

🐇 Rabbit moms and dads do not stay together after the babies are born.

🐇 Rabbits work as a team to build their tunnels.

🐇 A warren in England was found with 1,027 entrance and exit holes, and more than 400 rabbits.

Here is my home

After they meet, Mom and Dad dig a big, cozy chamber where we will be born. This is our nest.

Shopping trip
Up on the surface, rabbits collect grass, feathers, and fur to make a soft nest.

Can you see the cozy bed Mom has made?

I'm on the lookout.

The warren is a safe place to live. Larger animals find it hard to **squeeze** through the tunnels.

Inside my family's nest

When I am born, my eyes are shut tight and I don't have any fur. We stay warm by huddling close together in the cozy nest Mom has built.

Day one... **day two...**

day three.

Now I'm two weeks old.

All grow bigger!

At first the bunnies are very weak. They can hardly move at all. But soon they can move around. After 10 days, they open their eyes.

Rock-a-bye bunny
When they are not eating, the babies sleep almost all of the time. Growing fast is very tiring.

After two weeks, the bunnies have thick fur and they spend more time awake.

I'm getting curious

After about three weeks, we like to run and jump around inside the warren. We can't wait to start exploring the big world outside.

Mother's milk

Mother rabbits feed their baby bunnies with milk. This is called nursing. The bunnies are fed only once each day.

Rabbit facts

🐰 Rabbits spend most of their day undeground. They come out to eat at sunset and at dawn.

🐰 Rabbits can hear many sounds that humans cannot.

🐰 The deepest warren tunnels ever found were dug 30 ft (10 m) underground.

Now the bunnies are full and sleepy.

I'm four weeks old

It's time for me to hop out of my burrow. My brothers and sisters and I stay close to the entrance, just in case we need to ZOooom back inside!

Rabbits' ears stick up high to listen for danger.

The warm sand is a comfy place for the rabbits to sit.

I'm so shy, I think I'll hide!

Be careful!

Outside the safety of the warren, the bunnies are always on the lookout for danger. Bunnies are a meal for animals like eagles, foxes, and weasels.

eagle

fox

We run back down the tunnel when we get scared!

The bunnies' eyes quickly get used to bright daylight.

I can find my own dinner

Now I am old enough to look for food on my own. Green, leafy plants are my favorite food. I find yummy plants to eat growing in fields and in gardens.

This looks like a good place to eat dinner.

Favorite food

Rabbits eat many different kinds of plants. Most rabbits love to eat dandelion and carrot leaves, hay, and parsley.

Dandelion

Rabbits don't eat snails!

Rabbits will eat leafy plants like this Swiss chard wherever they find them— even in your garden!

Now I'm grown up

After just eight weeks, I am all grown up. I spend my time running in the fields, looking for good things to eat. Soon it will be time to start a family of my own.

Rabbits smell plants to see if they are good to eat.

Bath time
Rabbits spend a lot of time washing their fur. This is called grooming.

The rabbits' noses tell them that these buttercups are not good to eat.

Family life
Adult rabbits live together in a group. When new rabbits are born, they stay in the group.

The circle of life goes around and around

Now you know how I turned into a grown-up rabbit.

Bye-bye, off I hop.

My friends from around the world

Can you see why this rabbit is called a Blue dwarf ?

The Jackrabbit lives in the desert. Its big ears help it to stay cool in the desert sun.

This Angora rabbit has a lot of fur, and even funny tufts of fur on the tips of its ears!

The mountain hare has huge feet, which help it to run in the snow.

My fluffy, furry rabbit friends come in all sizes and colors.

Dutch rabbits are one of the most popular pet rabbits. They are known for being very gentle.

Lop-eared rabbits have ears that flop down to the ground.

The tiny pika is the size of a hamster!

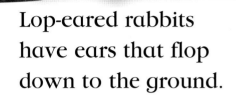

The Lion-head rabbit has a mane of fur on top of its head.

The Mountain hare is white so its enemies can't see it in the snow.

Rabbit facts

🐰 A rabbit's teeth grow throughout its entire life. Rabbits need to chew wood to keep their teeth short.

🐰 When rabbits are happy, they like to hop and jump around.

🐰 Rabbits are the most active at dawn and at twilight.

Glossary

Warren
A system of underground tunnels that rabbits live in.

Claw
A sharp nail on the rabbit's toe that helps the rabbit to dig.

Nest
A place inside the warren where rabbit babies are born.

Kitten
The name for a baby rabbit that is less than one month old.

Litter
A group of baby rabbits all born to the same mother.

Grooming
When the rabbit washes its fur to keep it clean and free of bugs.

Acknowledgments

The publisher would like to thank the following for their kind permission to reproduce their photographs:

(Key: a=above; c=centre; b=below; l=left; r=right; t=top)

1 Warren Photographic: Jane Burton c, bl. 2-3 Bruce Coleman Ltd: William S. Paton bkg&c. 2 DK Images: Jane Burton b. 3 Oxford Scientific Films: Jorge Sierra Antinolo br. 4-5 DK Images: Geoff Dann. 4 DK Images: Dave King l; Steven Moore Photography r; Bruce Coleman Ltd: William S. Paton b. 5 Bruce Coleman Ltd: William S. Paton br; FLPA - Images of nature: David Hosking tr; Steven Moore Photography tl; Warren Photographic: Jane Burton bl. 6-7 Corbis: Terry W. Eggers t; DK Images: Steve Shott b; 6 DK Images: Steve Shott c; Jane Burton cr; Bruce Coleman Ltd: Colin Varndell bl. 7 Corbis: Phillip Gould tc. 8-9 Corbis: Terry W. Eggers t; DK Images: Steve Shott b. 8 Corbis: Phillip Gould; Oxford Scientific Films cl. 9 DK Images: Steve Shott tlb. 10-11 Oxford Scientific Films. 10 Bruce Coleman Ltd: Jane Burton tl, c; Warren Photographic: Jane Burton tr. 11 Bruce Coleman Ltd: Jane Burton tr. 12 DK Images: Steve Shott l. 12-13 Oxford Scientific Films: Maurice Tibbles.

14-15 Bruce Coleman Ltd: William S. Paton. 15 DK Images: Frank Greenaway rca; Jerry Young rc; Oxford Scientific Films: br. 16-17 Steven Moore Photography. 16 DK Images: Ian O'Leary l; FLPA - Images of nature: Tony Hamblin br. 17 Royalty Free Images: Photofrenetic/ Alamy tr; DK Images: Jacqui Hurst br. 18-19 Bruce Coleman Ltd: Colin Varndell. 18 FLPA - Images of nature: Tony Hamblin br. 19 Oxford Scientific Films: Mike Powles tr. 20 Bruce Coleman Ltd: Jane Burton tc, trb; Corbis: Tony Hamblin bl; DK Images: Barrie Watts bc; Geoff Dann tl; Jane Burton cl; Warren Photographic: Jane Burton tr, cr, crb, c. 21 Steven Moore Photography bkg; Oxford Scientific Films: Jorge Sierra Antinolo c. 22 DK Images: Jane Burton tl; Steve Shott cl; Oxford Scientific Films: Paul Berquist tr; Warren Photographic: Jane Burton c. 22-23 Powerstock: Superstock. 23 Corbis: George D. Lepp trb; DK Images: Steve Shott tr; FLPA - Images of nature: Terry Whittaker cla; Steven Moore Photography: br; Warren Photographic: Jane Burton cl. 24 Bruce Coleman Ltd: Jane Burton cr, bl; DK Images: Steve Shott tl, cl; Steven Moore Photography: tr.

All other images © Dorling Kindersley.

For further information see: www.dkimages.com